STUDY-AID

Notes on Shak

TROILUS AND CRESSIDA

Compiled by
H. M. Burton, M.A. (Cantab.)

Methuen Educational Ltd
LONDON · TORONTO · SYDNEY · WELLINGTON

First published in 1975 by Methuen Educational Ltd
11 New Fetter Lane, London EC4P 4EE

Printed in Great Britain by Fletcher & Son Ltd, Norwich

ISBN 0 423 88940 0

NOTE: These Notes are published for use as an aid to the study of English Literature for examination purposes. It is important to remember that the Notes serve only as an aid to the study of the book and do not in any way relieve the student of the necessity of reading the original text.

Contents

I Shakespeare's life and works

William Shakespeare was christened in the prosperous market-town of Stratford-on-Avon, Warwickshire, on 26 April, 1564; traditionally, his actual birthday was three days earlier, on St George's Day, the same day as his death fifty-two years later. His father, John, was a respected middle-class trader, and his mother, Mary Arden, came from a family of local landowners. It seems probable that young William received a fair education (for his day) at the local Grammar School; at the age of eighteen he married a girl eight years older than himself, Anne Hathaway, who gave him a child the following year and twins in 1585. Little else is known of his early life, and so we cannot tell what made him decide to leave Stratford in 1586 for London, where he stayed until 1611. In London he must soon have attracted attention because by 1592 he was popular enough a writer and actor to be sneered at by an older dramatist as an uneducated jack-of-all-trades. He is mentioned as being among the principal actors of the city as early as 1598, and in 1599 we find that he is a member of the company running the Globe Theatre, with one-tenth interest in the profits – showing a business sense rarely seen in his fellow writers. His popularity is indicated by the fact that not only were his own plays published under his name (a rare procedure in his day) but also plays by others are to be found attributed to him, as if to indicate that his name alone would guarantee a good sale. An anthology of contemporary literature published in 1598 lists all of his plays (up to that date) and places him at the head of his contemporaries. Shakespeare must have been careful with his money; he bought up property in his home town, including the second biggest house in Stratford, where in 1611, again for no known reason, he retired to live the life of a rich country gentleman till his death in 1616.

Shakespeare's genius: With Shakespeare, more perhaps than with any other writer, our ignorance of his life and opinions matters very little; in his best plays we need make no allowances for him, but are presented with an almost godlike insight into a number of different types of person, and can only wonder how one man can have known so much about so many, and have shown it without the least revelation of his own personality. It is best to forget our ignorance of his character and of much of his life and instead to concentrate on his works. These may conveniently be divided into five more or less chronological groups.

1. Apprenticeship 1586–1593: It is difficult to establish a firm date for Shakespeare's early plays; the evidence is scanty and often conflicting and in any case it is possible – or even probable – that he wrote only parts of the earliest plays which are usually included in his collected works. One of the most popular types of drama at the end of the sixteenth century was the chronicle play, a sort of 'real life' drama written around events which were still alive, if not exactly fresh, in the minds of people who went to see plays. The Wars of the Roses, for example, had been over for more than a century, but histories and stories and ballads had kept them in the public memory, just as in our own day the public interest in the events and incidents of the First World War seems to be as keen as it was nearly sixty years ago. It is not surprising, therefore, that playwrights and theatre managers, looking round for subjects to attract the public, turned to these wars which had torn England apart so tragically in the previous century. Shakespeare had read some at least of the history books, but he knew that in any case his audience would be familiar with the main 'stories' and the principal characters.

The first play in which his hand is clearly recognizable is *Henry VI, Part I.* (Some critics believe that it is nearly all Shakespeare's handiwork; others that he wrote only parts of it.) It was probably written in 1589–1590 and produced in 1591. The Second and Third Parts of *Henry VI* followed in quick succession. Other early plays include *Love's Labour's Lost* (1591) – a rich and elegant comedy which is apparently wholly Shakespeare's – two comedies [*A Comedy of Errors* (about 1591) and *Two Gentlemen of Verona* (1591–1592)] based on Latin plays by Plautus and a gory tragedy, also based on Roman origins, *Titus Andronicus* (1593–1594), with some fine Shakespearean passages among the horrors. It was typical of the age, when the theatre was expanding rapidly but new and original plays were hard to come by, that as a change from chronicle plays the playwrights, of whom Shakespeare was only one, should turn to the Classics for ideas; after all, they had studied these works at school and university and the best plays and stories were already known to many in their audiences.

2. Growing success 1593–1599: It is unwise to think that Shakespeare divided his professional life into definite periods or that his works can similarly be placed in water-tight compartments. For example, *Richard III* and *King John* (both about 1593) belong chronologically, and partly in content, to his 'Apprenticeship' period yet both show many signs of growing maturity. But when, in 1594, he became one of 'The Lord Chamberlain's Men', the leading theatrical company of the day, his apprenticeship was surely finished and he was firmly set on the road to success. With colleagues like Richard Burbage, the great tragic actor, and Will Kempe, the most popular comic actor, he was among the top artists in their profession and was inspired to write at his most brilliant. (He was even happy to play small parts on the stage with them.) Comedies like *As You Like It* and *Twelfth Night*, histories like *Richard II*, *Henry IV* and *Henry V* and tragedies like *Romeo and Juliet* and *Julius Caesar* flowed from his brain and his pen in an astonishing succession. It was one of the most excitingly productive few years in the history of the theatre. It saw not only the production of some of the most popular plays, like *A Midsummer Night's Dream* and *The Merchant of Venice*, but the creation of some of the most famous (and best-loved) characters, from Bottom to Shylock, from Sir Toby Belch to Beatrice and Benedict, from Falstaff to King Henry V.

From this period, too, the boundaries between types of drama were becoming blurred. There is a growing awareness that, in the words of a later writer, life is a 'tangled skein'. There are hints of something approaching tragedy in comedies like *The Merchant of Venice* and *Much Ado About Nothing* and there is rich comedy in some of the Histories. Shakespeare's growing interest in his characters, and his deeper appreciation of the subtleties in human nature as a whole, are reflected in the general broadening of his ideas on what makes a successful and moving play. *Richard II* (1593), for example, could almost be a sketch for *Hamlet* (1602–1603) and the Antony of *Julius Caesar* (1599) foreshadows the Antony of *Antony and Cleopatra* (1607–1608).

3. The tragic phase 1599–1608: In 1599 Shakespeare's company acquired the famous Globe Theatre, the biggest public theatre in England at that time; in 1603, when Queen Elizabeth died, the Lord Chamberlain's Men became the King's Men under the generous patronage of James I, and were as successful at court as they were with the public. The plays of this period include the great tragedies, *Macbeth*, *Othello*, *King Lear* and *Hamlet*, the Roman plays, *Julius Caesar*, *Coriolanus* and *Antony and Cleopatra*, and what are sometimes called the 'problem plays', *Timon of Athens*, *Troilus and Cressida*, *All's Well that Ends Well* and *Measure for Measure*. In all of them we see ideas from earlier plays developed with a sureness and mastery which is phenomenal, with less emphasis on characterization (although the characters are still supremely well created and developed) and more on imagery and themes. The 'problem plays' are so called because, while drawing on the traditional schools of comedy, tragedy and history, they do not fall clearly into any of these categories. Shakespeare's vision of humanity, it has been said, was too far-ranging to be simple, and for these plays especially no generalization will suffice to explain the nature of that vision.

4. The last plays 1608–1611: In 1608 the King's Men bought a new theatre, the Blackfriars, which was more comfortable and expensive and, above all, indoors; although performances continued at the Globe until it was burnt down (traditionally on the first night of *Henry VIII*) the last plays seem to require the cosier and relatively luxurious atmosphere of the 'private' indoor theatre. Apart from *Henry VIII*, which was written in collaboration with another playwright, the last four plays, *Pericles, Cymbeline, The Winter's Tale* and *The Tempest,* form a remarkable unity and a fitting close to the dramatist's career. In all of them bold use is made of devices which in a lesser writer would seem farcical, and many critics have found that the demands they make on the reader's credulity and imagination are excessive. But it is well to remind ourselves that they were not written to be *read* and the skill of Shakespeare can inspire that 'willing suspension of disbelief' in things seen on the stage which the reader finds it more difficult to achieve. In any case, these four plays present a vision of beauty and harmony, in which suffering gives way to forgiveness, and misfortune to joy and reconciliation, presented in a form of poetical drama which, for all its subtlety, is an expression of the direct and simple truths of human affections and their magic.

From then till now: For over two centuries after his death, Shakespeare's genius was admired by the critics and neglected by the theatre, which was happy to rewrite, to 'improve' and 'polish' his plays into something more closely resembling contemporary theatre. In our own century we have seen a reaction against this state of affairs, with a resurgence of interest in his plays *as* plays, and with striking and original attempts to bring together the discoveries of scholarship and the experience of the theatre-goer.

5. Shakespeare's poetry: Even in his least 'great' plays Shakespeare showed that in his command of the language, his verbal inventiveness and imagery, his natural instinctive power to 'charm' the listener, he was perhaps above all else a poet. It was, in fact, as a poet that he set out – or almost. In 1593 he published his long poem *Venus and Adonis*, and in his Preface, addressed to the Earl of Southampton, he described it as 'the first heir of my invention'. This does not necessarily mean that it was his first written work; plays written to be performed were in a different class from books written to be read; in any case much of his work for the theatre hitherto had been editing, adaptation and a kind of 'writing to order' rather than sheer invention. In 1594 another long poem appeared, *The Rape of Lucrece,* also dedicated to the Earl of Southampton. That these poems were widely read and enjoyed (more, probably, than they are today) is shown by the fact that in Shakespeare's lifetime, seven editions of the first were issued and five of the second.

Some years later, in 1609, were published his *Sonnets,* and there is some reason to think that they were published without his permission. They were strictly personal poems but scholars all over the world have never established beyond a doubt either the identity of the people obscurely referred to in many of them or the person or persons to whom they were addressed. They vary in poetic quality but the finest of them reveal the same wisdom, the same depth of thought and the same supreme command of language that we find in the finest of his dramatic writing.

Finally we cannot ignore Shakespeare as a lyric poet. He lived in an age when people from every walk of life *sang* and his many songs reflect the passion for poetical words set to beautiful melodies, sad, sentimental, happy or merely narrative. Even Milton, a genius of a very different cast of mind, wrote affectionately, some fifteen or sixteen years after Shakespeare's death, of 'sweetest Shakespeare, Fancy's child' warbling 'his native wood-notes wild'.

II Suggestions on reading Shakespeare

When studying Shakespeare it is vital to remember that his plays were originally written not to be read but to be performed, that they contain a great deal of poetry, and that, because they were written more than 350 years ago, they contain some allusions with which we are not familiar and some words which we no longer use. Apart from these difficulties, they may be read as any other play: for the story, the characters, and the ideas about life which they present.

Dramatic reconstruction: It is the job of the director, the producer and the actors to reconstruct the printed play, the words on the page, into the performance on the stage. Where no such stage performance is available – and *Troilus and Cressida* is seldom performed publicly – the student or the reader must do this reconstruction for himself (or herself) *in the imagination*. It becomes more necessary, in fact, to imagine the dialogue being spoken, the reactions of any other characters present, even the scenery and properties (if any). We do this, subconsciously of course, when we are reading a novel; but a novel is written to be read and the writer has usually done his best to help the imagination. With a play, a more conscious effort is required and it is not easy to sustain; but it is worth the effort. This technique – which the reader comes to apply almost without effort in time – not only goes a long way to familiarizing the reader with the details of the action; it also enables him to 'get inside' the characters themselves and to understand their motives and personalities.

Re-reading and memorizing: It is impossible to lay down any rule in this matter. Some students will want to re-read some scenes over and over again, partly because they feel that such scenes cannot be fully grasped without many re-readings, partly because they enjoy certain scenes more than any others. The same is true about memorizing; some speeches seem to cry out to be learnt by heart; they are dramatically and poetically superb pieces of writing and add to the possessions of a richly filled mind. Other students are less impressed by the 'set pieces'; they prefer to memorize a few short speeches, even single lines – although these often stay in the memory without being purposely memorized. (Who can forget Troilus's trenchant line in Act two, scene two: 'What's aught but as 'tis valued? '?)

One thing, however, is certain. It is advisable – even compulsory – to read straight through a Shakespeare play once! Such a rapid reading will leave many points unclear, many words and phrases unexplained; but it will give the reader the elements of the story. A second reading will give opportunities to get a firmer hold of the structure of the play, the details of the plot, the importance of the various characters. All will now be ready for the *detailed* study – the imagery, the variations of tone, the personalities involved, the allusions and the difficult words and phrases.

Character analysis: In the mature Shakespeare, what happens in the play usually has its roots in the characters. Things happen as they do because the characters are what they are. How may the characters be analysed?

> Human beings reveal themselves by what they say, by their manner of saying it, and often enough by their silence or their failure to say anything in the given circumstances.
>
> We can learn about people, too, by their actions, and even by their failure to act on occasions.
>
> We know them, also, from what others say about them.
>
> It is sometimes possible to confirm or qualify our assessment of characters by a slightly artificial device, that of considering two characters together and comparing or contrasting them. This device, however, popular as it is with the writers of school texts of Shakespeare, can be dangerous if it isolates the 'chosen pair' from the general current of the play. It is most useful, perhaps, when two characters *appear* usually as a pair, like Dogberry and Verges in *Much Ado About Nothing* or Helena and Hermia in *A Midsummer Night's Dream*. There is little scope for it in *Troilus and Cressida*, except perhaps for Thersites and Pandarus.

Obscure allusions and language: There is no quick way round these difficulties. A good students' edition of the play will contain Notes and a Glossary (see the Reading List on page 44). Modern educational and literary opinion, however, tends to the theory that the importance of these difficulties has been exaggerated and we no longer see editions in which the Notes and Glossary fill far more pages than the text of the play. For the scholar there are the established (and admirable) texts, which sometimes take a page or more to comment on something which is either obvious or unimportant; for the ordinary reader or student there are editions like the *Signet* or the *Temple*, with full glossaries but minimal Notes.

III General introduction to the play

Date of publication

Apparently there were two versions of Shakespeare's *Troilus and Cressida* – three, if one includes the First Folio version. The first was authorized to be printed in 1603, when it was described: 'as yt is acted by my Lord Chamberlens men'. This was Shakespeare's company and his name is included in the authorization to print. But this version was not after all printed. In 1609, however, a Quarto edition was published, and an extra leaf was added before publication which included an address to the reader. The original title-page of this quarto stated that 'it was acted by the King's maiesties seruants at the Globe' – although this statement was removed when the address to the reader was inserted. The King's Men, as we have seen, was the company formerly known as The Lord Chamberlain's Men, so we are left wondering whether the reference applies to that performance in 1603 or to a fresh production in 1609. It does not matter very much because in 1623 *Troilus and Cressida* was one of the plays printed in the First Folio. There are numerous errors in the Folio, but that is true of nearly all the plays included; the point is that the Folio version is substantially the same as the 1609 quarto.

There are practically no references to any public performances of this play until the twentieth century. This is not surprising; there are few of the 'popular' elements of Shakespearean drama in *Troilus and Cressida*: little humour, no single great tragic or comic central figure, no really prominent part for a great actress, no graceful lyrics. It has been suggested, in fact, that even in Shakespeare's own day it was performed only for a sophisticated and highly educated body of lawyers.

Sources

One thing we can be certain of: Shakespeare's audience knew *something* about the Trojan War. They were even more familiar with the story of Troilus and Cressida. Those who could read had the choice of versions by Homer (in translation), Chaucer (about 1382), Lydgate (1412–1420), Caxton (about 1470), Henryson (fifteenth century) and others; those who could not read must have heard the story told and sung from their childhood. Shakespeare scarcely had to 'read up' any of these works but he probably – even subconsciously – drew on all of them. There had even been an earlier play, now lost, by Dekker and Chettle, of the same title – produced in 1599 and no doubt well known by Shakespeare.

Scholars are divided on the extent to which Shakespeare 'borrowed' from his sources. American critics tend to emphasize the influence of Homer (in Chapman's famous translation), Lydgate and Henryson; in England, Dover Wilson was inclined to think that Shakespeare acquired most of the facts he needed 'from the schoolroom'. The influence of Chaucer's lovely poem is problematical, mainly because Shakespeare's Cressida, popularly regarded in his day as a loose young woman, even a harlot, is a very different character from Chaucer's.

For the average reader or student there is really no problem here. Shakespeare's so-called 'sources' were seldom more than a starting-point or, alternatively, a convenient store-house to be raided when the opportunity arose. He might 'lift' whole passages from Plutarch and mould them into blank verse (as in *Antony and Cleopatra*, for example), or he might seize upon a serious story from some Italian novelist and use it as a skeleton on which to build a light-hearted comedy. What is important is what he did with his 'sources'. If his conception of the dramatic possibilities of the story – possibilities perhaps overlooked by the original author – required a character to be changed into something quite different, he would think nothing of making the change; even in his historical plays he might shift an incident backward or forward in time by a few years if this would add to the dramatic effect. It all makes a fascinating, and indeed important, study – for scholars; for the ordinary reader or student it is, in the end, the finished article, the play that Shakespeare wrote, which matters most.

What is the play about

This is not as simple as it is with most Shakespeare plays because it is 'about' two different things which are not at all skilfully intertwined but rather run side by side. Neither of the two themes can be regarded as the main plot, neither as a sub-plot.

One theme is the Trojan War, but the picture it suggests of the ten-year conflict is not clear. The 'commanders' on the two sides, Greek and Trojan, appear to be on almost friendly terms and the discussions among themselves, especially among the Greeks, seem more bitter than their hostility toward the enemy.

The other theme, which gives the play its title, is the love of Troilus, a Trojan and one of King Priam's sons, and Cressida, the daughter of a Trojan 'priest' who has gone over to the Greeks.

Only in the rather hectic last Act do these two themes come closely together, although even here there is little attempt to combine them as parts of the same story. Shakespeare seems to have been experimenting with the idea of portraying inconstancy and inconsistency, in public affairs and in private affairs, in one and the same play – as he did so triumphantly in the great tragedies. But for reasons we can only conjecture his heart was not in it and the experiment was not a success.

The players

Although more detailed remarks on the characters appear in subsequent sections of these Notes, it is essential at the outset for the student to become familiar with the main characters.

Troilus, one of the sons of Priam, King of Troy. He is in love with Cressida, who, however, is 'exchanged' for a Trojan prisoner. When she joins the Greek camp she is at once 'wooed and won' by Diomedes, a Greek commander. Troilus vows revenge and there seems to have been one encounter between them as a result of which Diomedes captures Troilus's horse. But the latter, although heart-broken, never succeeds in exacting his revenge.

Achilles, the most distinguished of the Greek commanders, although his part in the play is disappointing. He spends much of his time 'sulking in his tent' but when his friend Patroclus is killed by Hector he comes out to meet Hector in single combat. He takes advantage of his opponent being unarmed and kills him. He then has Hector's body tied to his horse's tail and drags him through the camp.

Hector, if there is a 'hero' in *Troilus and Cressida* it is Hector. He shows a strange mixture of statesmanship and chivalry, both in his speech and in his actions. As the Trojan hero he fights Ajax but breaks off when he remembers that Ajax is his nephew, and later is preparing to fight Achilles when he is treacherously killed.

Ajax, a Greek commander, although a nephew of Trojan Hector (another example of the lack of definition between the two sides in the Trojan War). He is obviously a little slow-witted and something of a butt, and is easily taken in by the flattery of Ulysses.

Ulysses, another Greek commander, and another disappointment. From his speeches he appears full of wisdom but he engages in almost childish conspiracies to arouse Achilles. At the end, he appears to befriend Troilus when the latter is in despair over the faithlessness of Cressida (although Ulysses and Troilus are actually enemies!) but from his comments he seems more sardonic than sympathetic.

Patroclus, one of the Greek commanders who is most important as the friend of Achilles, whom he can obviously amuse but who resists his attempts to persuade him to fight in the war again. It was when Hector

killed Patroclus that Achilles finally took up arms – to kill Hector.
Thersites, 'A deformed and scurrilous Greek'. Achilles 'spoils' him and allows him to give tongue to his cynicism and his obsession with 'lechery, lechery'.
Pandarus, he is Cressida's uncle and acts as 'pander' in her love affair with Troilus.
Cressida, the only female character of any importance. Her father, Calchas, was a Trojan who had gone over to the Greeks. It is when she rejoins him that she shows her faithlessness to Troilus.
Cassandra, a daughter of Priam and so sister of the Trojan commanders. She prophesies doom on her rare appearances and foretells Hector's death.

(The other 'minor' characters, are dealt with in section eight.)

IV Historical background

Strictly speaking, there is none! Historians agree that there *was* a Trojan War, which lasted for ten years, but that is as far as any will go with confidence. Since it took place possibly at some time between 1400 B.C. and 1100 B.C. and there are no records which go so far back, this is not surprising. Even Homer – if he existed – who wrote about the Trojan War in the *Iliad* – assuming Homer wrote the *Iliad* – was writing at least a hundred years after the War, and possibly four hundred. ('Writing' is probably the wrong word anyway. Scholars believe that the works attributed to Homer were more likely a collection of songs and poems, perhaps put into some order by 'Homer' but not written down for a century or more afterwards.)

It was not unnatural for Greece to go to war with Troy because the latter stood at the tip of the Hellespont and so guarded the route to the Black Sea – where the Greeks were anxious to trade. But Homer gives a more romantic explanation. The *Iliad* deals with the last phase of the Trojan War but its origins are clearly and frequently referred to. Apparently Paris, one of the sons of Priam, King of Troy, on a visit to Sparta, fell in love with Helen, the wife of Menelaus, the King of Sparta. Whether she was equally in love with Paris is not clear – although she apparently lived quite happily with him in Troy for ten years – but in any case she ran away with him. Menelaus, who had been the most successful among the many noble suitors for Helen's hand, gathered together all the disappointed suitors, collected a large navy and set out to recapture his wife. (Faustus, in Marlowe's tragedy, when given a vision of Helen, said 'Was this the face that launched a thousand ships? ')

But the bare bones of Homer's narrative were thickly overlaid with additional legends throughout the Middle Ages. The famous Trojan Horse, for example, is not in Homer; nor is the story of Troilus and Cressida. As we have seen, there were at least six versions of the story which Shakespeare might have drawn upon, not including the songs and ballads and stories which have not survived. Indeed, the firm hold on the imagination of the twelfth to the fifteenth century in Europe is one of the most astonishing features of literature. In the West it can only be compared with the *Roland* stories and the Arthurian legends.

This is why there is no historical background to *Troilus and Cressida*, except in so far as the piling of legend upon legend is, or was, a historical phenomenon. Perhaps we should speak rather of the *literary* background.

V Brief outline of the plot

As we have seen, there is no 'plot', in the accepted sense, in *Troilus and Cressida*, no controlled series of linked scenes which carry on the story and bring it to a satisfactory conclusion. Instead, there are two themes, not closely linked, which are still left with loose ends at the final curtain. The development of these themes can be roughly traced, act by act, but will be more closely examined in the next section.

Act One: In the first two scenes we are introduced to Troilus and to Cressida and, at least by name and partly by reputation, to some of the Trojan heroes. Troilus appears as the ardent lover, Cressida as the cool spectator, Pandarus as the go-between.

In scene three the Greek commanders are shown in conference and we begin to see their different qualities. A challenge arrives from Hector to meet any Greek in single combat.

Act Two: Most of scenes one and three are concerned with Hector's challenge and with the feelings aroused in the Greek camp by Achilles' ill-humoured withdrawal from all physical action. Between these scenes we are shown the Trojans in conference (as a sort of balance to the Greeks' conference in act one) and are given a puzzling glimpse of Hector's character and temperament.

Act Three: Cressida re-enters the story in this act. We hear more of Troilus's love for her and by the end of the second scene Cressida has also declared herself, and Pandarus triumphantly arranges the final bringing together of the lovers. In the third scene we hear that Cressida is to be returned to her father in the Greek camp in exchange for a prisoner of war. We also see the Greek commanders trying to snub Achilles and we learn that it is to be Ajax who is to meet Hector in single combat.

Act Four: A sort of filling-in or marking-time act in which both 'themes' are advanced a stage further. Diomedes arrives to fetch Cressida and there is a parting scene between her and Troilus. In the last scene of the act the promised single combat takes place, but turns out to be a fiasco. Meanwhile Cressida has arrived in the Greek camp.

Act Five: 'Things happen' in this act. Cressida deserts Troilus in favour of Diomedes; Achilles decides against fighting Hector because of a letter he has received; Troilus fights Diomedes, but apparently inconclusively; Hector goes about looking for somebody to fight and while resting, unarmed, he is slain by Achilles' myrmidons.

VI Summary of the play

Act One

Scene one Troilus speaks of his love for Cressida but Pandarus (Cressida's uncle) grows tired of his ecstasies and threatens to cease his efforts to encourage his niece. Troilus, left alone, remarks on the folly of the war over Helen, who cannot be compared with Cressida. He is interrupted by Aeneas, a Trojan officer, with whom he departs for the battle-field.

Scene two In a street in Troy, Alexander, Cressida's servant, tells her how Hector, one of Troilus's brothers, is (untypically) angry because he has been 'struck down' in battle by Ajax, a Greek commander, whom he despises. Pandarus enters. He sings Troilus's praises but Cressida pretends to be completely unmoved. As the Trojan leaders return from the battle-field, Pandarus points them out one by one to Cressida; when Troilus appears, Pandarus becomes even more lyrical, especially when Cressida pretends to admire a Greek hero, Achilles, above Troilus. Troilus's boy then comes in to summon Pandarus to his master and when she is alone again Cressida admits that she is already attracted to Troilus but is determined to 'hold off', on the principle that 'Men prize the thing ungained more than it is'.

Scene three In the Greek camp, Agamemnon, Nestor, Menelaus and Ulysses are in conference. If it is supposed to be a council of war it sounds at first more like a mutual admiration society. Then Ulysses, in the long and famous speech on 'degree', explains why in his opinion the war has dragged on for years without success. The Greeks, he says, have lost discipline and a sense of purpose. Achilles lies in his tent, laughing at empty jokes and encouraging Patroclus to parody the greatness of the Greek leaders.

They are interrupted by Aeneas, from Troy, who brings a challenge from Hector, a Trojan hero and a brother of Troilus, to engage in single combat with any Greek they care to nominate. The natural choice would have been Achilles, but after Agamemnon has left with Aeneas and the Greek lords, Ulysses stays behind with Nestor to discuss a plan he has thought of. He points out that if Hector were to defeat Achilles it would be a bitter blow to the Greeks and if he won it would only increase Achilles' pride and conceit. Instead, he suggests, let 'blockish Ajax' be chosen to oppose Hector. Nestor agrees: he obviously sees that Ulysses' plot is directed not so much at defeating Hector as at annoying Achilles.

Act Two

Scene one After a 'slanging match' between Ajax and Thersites ('a deformed and scurrilous Greek') Achilles and Patroclus enter and try to pacify them. But the quarrel continues until Thersites goes off, when Achilles announces that the proclamation, about which Ajax had been trying to question Thersites, is to the effect that Hector has challenged any Greek to single combat. Achilles dismisses the challenge as 'trash'. When asked who is to meet the challenge, he says 'I know not. 'Tis put to lottery' – but we know that the lottery will be 'rigged'.

Scene two We are back in Troy, at King Priam's palace. The king and his sons are discussing a suggestion from the Greeks that the Trojans should give up Helen and put an end to this stupid war. Helenus and Hector are in favour of the idea; Troilus is indignantly against, supported, not surprisingly, by Paris. A brief interruption by the mad Cassandra, prophesying woe, does nothing to affect the argument. After her departure Hector seems to change sides. Although he still maintains that Helen is lawfully Menelaus's wife he thinks that to surrender her now would be a blow to their 'joint and several dignities'.

(Note Troilus's interjection in line fifty-two – 'What's aught, but as 'tis valued? ' – in its way a cynical or satirical comment on the whole tone of the play.)

Scene three Thersites, who left the scene before Achilles' tent in the first scene of this Act, is back again, railing against Ajax and Achilles. The latter calls him into his tent but he doesn't go, but first Patroclus and then Achilles himself come out for him. The three of them indulge in some trivial word-play, in which Thersites reminds one of the typical Shakespearean clown – except that Thersites seems obsessed with the subject of lechery. When they see Agamemnon approaching, with three or four other Greek leaders, Achilles retreats to his tent, saying 'I'll speak with nobody' and Thersites follows him, leaving Patroclus to confront the Greek leaders. They ask for Achilles and send Patroclus in to bring him out. Patroclus returns, but without Achilles, who sends smooth messages. Agamemnon sends him back, with instructions to tell Achilles that they are tired of his sulky inaction. This time Ulysses goes in with Patroclus and in their absence Agamemnon flatters Ajax by assuring him that he is every bit as good a man as Achilles, without Achilles' pride.

Ulysses returns with the news that Achilles will not leave his tent to come to the battle-field. The general theory is that he is too proud. Ajax blusters a good deal, but the other commanders, by flattery (and by revealing asides to each other and to the audience) pacify him and at the same time show how they despise him.

Act Three

Scene one In Priam's palace in Troy, Pandarus is talking to a servant of Paris and once again we are reminded of Shakespeare's clowns as Pandarus and the servant 'tease' each other like Rosalind and Touchstone in *As You Like It* or Viola and Feste in *Twelfth Night*. Pandarus seizes the opportunity to sing the praises of Cressida (and to remind the audience of her existence!). Paris enters, with Helen, and after a rather dull argument in which Pandarus fails to interest the lovers in the affair of Cressida, he sings a rather tepid love-song. (It is worth noting that in this scene Paris shows that after ten years or so he is still apparently in love with Helen!) He asks Helen to come with him to help disarm Hector.

Scene two In Pandarus's orchard Troilus, in most poetic language, tells of his infatuation for Cressida while Pandarus has gone to fetch her. He returns with her but withdraws almost at once. Cressida appears to have some fears for the future but after Pandarus has come back to see how they are getting on she grows bolder and declares her real love for Troilus. Pandarus is of course delighted with the success of his plan and sends the lovers indoors, where he has prepared a room and a bed for them.

Scene three Already the shadow of tragedy falls on Troilus's happiness, although he is not yet aware of it. We are with the Greeks again and Calchas is addressing Agamemnon and the 'princes'. Apparently Calchas, a Trojan priest, who has changed sides and has done some service for the Greeks, is seeking his reward. Agamemnon asks what he wants and Calchas requests that his daughter Cressida, still in Troy, should be returned to him in exchange for a prisoner, Antenor, taken only the day before. The Trojans value him very highly and will be quite willing to release Cressida in exchange for him. Agamemnon agrees and sends one of his commanders, Diomedes, to Troy to effect the exchange.

The scene shifts, although we are still in scene three, to outside Achilles' tent. The other Greek commanders see him and decide to snub him by walking past him and refusing to acknowledge him or to talk to him. Ulysses, however, does stay. He speaks frankly to Achilles – especially in the great speech beginning, 'Time hath, my lord, a wallet at his back'. Greatness must be kept alive, he says, in people's minds; it will not live on unless sustained. The new will oust the old, as an arriving guest is welcomed warmly while the departing guest is perfunctorily dismissed. Even Ajax (who is to fight Hector) will displace Achilles. Moreover, he adds, everybody knows that Achilles is in love with Polyxena, a Trojan princess and a sister of Hector. After Ulysses has gone, Thersites reports (with much fooling and word-play) that Ajax is preparing to fight next day with Hector and Achilles sends Patroclus and Thersites with a letter asking Hector to meet him, unarmed, after the duel.

Act Four

Scene one Although there are references to a long-standing bitterness between Aeneas and Diomedes, the main purpose of this scene is to bring in Diomedes with Agamemnon's proposal to exchange Antenor for Cressida. Diomedes' closing speeches present an extremely sour Greek opinion of Helen, but it is not clear how far Diomedes speaks for the Greeks as a whole. It may well be, as Paris asserts, that Diomedes, as merchants (chapmen) do, is trying to bring down the value of something the Greeks want to buy.

Scene two Troilus and Cressida have had their night of love and now Aeneas comes to break the news that Cressida is to be exchanged for Antenor and she must return to her father. Troilus goes out to meet the delegation and Cressida, declaring that she will never go, is consumed with rather melodramatic grief.

Scene three A very brief scene in which Troilus tells Paris that he will fetch Cressida at once.

Scene four The parting of Troilus and Cressida is full of irony. She pleads undying love for Troilus, while he is restrained, his language is poetic and full of imagery but outwardly he seems well under control, as though he suspects that if he abandons himself to grief he will make things even harder for Cressida. When Diomedes comes to fetch her – and note that he is accompanied by *Trojan* lords – Troilus threatens to cut his throat if Cressida is not well used by the Greeks. But Shakespeare's audience, or most of them, knew that Cressida would not keep her solemn vows to Troilus and Troilus would never cut Diomedes' throat.

Scene five The lists are set out for the combat between Hector and Ajax. The trumpet is sounded but is not answered. Diomedes enters with Cressida and the Greek commanders welcome her, each with a kiss. Only

Menelaus and Ulysses refrain, the former because apparently he is no longer interested in kissing since he lost Helen (Patroclus has 'one for Menelaus' as well as one for himself) and Ulysses apparently because he thinks nothing of Cressida. (When she has gone, in fact, he more or less condemns her as one of the 'daughters of the game'.) A Trojan trumpet sounds and the combat is about to begin. There has been some talk about Ajax being Hector's nephew and nobody is surprised when Diomedes stops the fight. Ajax would have liked to continue but Hector says he will not fight his 'father's sister's son'. So instead of a mortal combat we get a kind of fraternization at top level in which the Greeks seem to vie with each other in praising the Trojan Hector, who, in turn, has nothing but respect and praise for the Greeks, especially Achilles. Finally, Achilles and Hector agree to fight the next day. The scene ends with Troilus asking Ulysses to take him to Calchas's tent.

Act Five

In most Shakespearean plays, comedies, tragedies or histories, this final act sees the resolving of problems, the clearing up of mysteries and the 'happy issue' or the death of the leading characters. In this play there are no straightforward *dénouements* but the author seems to be trying hard to give the acceptable ending to his play. It doesn't quite work; there is much bustling about and many changes of scene, but in the end nothing is satisfactorily settled.

Scene one Thersites brings Achilles a letter. While he is reading it Thersites has a vitriolic conversation with Patroclus – obviously to fill in the gap while Achilles is reading. The letter is from Queen Hecuba in Troy, reminding him of his vows to Polyxena, her daughter (and therefore Hector's sister), and Achilles' mistress (see act three, scene three). He uses the letter as an excuse to withdraw from the combat with Hector. He takes Patroclus back into the tent, leaving Thersites to rail against the Greeks. He is interrupted by Agamemnon and his 'staff', looking for Achilles. The latter takes Hector, Ajax and Nestor into his tent and the others go their several ways. Ulysses tells Troilus that Diomedes is on his way to Calchas's tent, advises him to follow and offers to go with him.

Scene two The scene shifts, in fact, to Calchas's tent. Diomedes enters looking for Cressida, who joins him at once. 'At a distance' Troilus approaches, with Ulysses and Thersites, and they remain concealed. Cressida pretends to resist the approaches of Diomedes but soon goes to fetch a 'pledge' – a sleeve to wear on his helmet. Troilus, watching his beloved promising herself to Diomedes, is torn with passion; Ulysses implores him to keep quiet and he promises again and again to do so, but his passion is too strong. Meanwhile Thersites throws in an occasional comment, usually scurrilous. After Cressida has gone, Troilus, almost demented, tries to argue that it was not Cressida he was watching – a Cressida, perhaps; Diomedes' Cressida; but not his, Troilus's, Cressida. Aeneas comes in to say he has been looking for Troilus everywhere. Hector is arming in the Trojan camp, and Ajax is on his way to conduct Troilus 'home' from the Greek camp.

Scene three Before Priam's tent Andromache, Hector's wife, and Cassandra, his sister, are trying to persuade him not to fight. Cassandra is sent to fetch Priam to add his pleas to theirs but Hector is adamant, even after Cassandra tells how she foresees Hector's death. Troilus, who has wandered in, supports Hector and declares that he will seek out Diomedes and win back his sleeve. Pandarus comes in with a letter from Cressida, which Troilus reads and then tears up.

Scene four The battle is now raging. Troilus and Diomedes cross the 'stage', fighting, leaving Thersites, who is challenged by Hector. When Thersites claims that he is no more than a 'rascal, a scurvy railing knave', Hector believes him – and spares him.

Scene five Diomedes comes on, with his servant. He has apparently had the better of the fight so far and captured Troilus's horse, which he sends to Cressida as witness that he is 'her knight'. Agamemnon enters with the news that the battle is going against them. The Trojans have brought up a fabulous monster, the sagittary (a centaur) which is terrifying the troops. He appeals to Diomedes to return to the battle. Then old Nestor arrives, with the body of Patroclus, which he despatches to Achilles. Hector is fighting fiercely and carrying all before him. Ulysses enters to encourage the Greeks with the news that Achilles is armed and, furious at the loss of Patroclus, is in the heart of the battle, with his myrmidons, roaring for Hector. Ajax makes a brief appearance, shouting for Troilus, who has also done great deeds. Finally Achilles himself comes in; he is determined to get Hector.

Scene six The battle is still raging. Ajax and Diomedes come looking for Troilus who, when he appears, takes both of them on. Hector arrives in time to see them all go off fighting and applauds his young brother.

Achilles enters and he and Hector at once start to fight. Hector sees that Achilles is tiring and offers to give him a rest. Achilles, although he affects to 'disdain' this 'courtesy', takes advantage of it and goes off. Troilus comes in, still bent on fighting recklessly, this time to rescue Aeneas, who has been taken by Ajax. Then enters 'one in sumptuous armour' who runs off when Hector challenges him, but Hector follows, determined to capture the armour!

Scene seven Achilles is on the field surrounded by his myrmidons. He instructs them to follow him, and when they meet Hector they are to surround him like a fence ('empale him with your weapons round about'). Paris and Menelaus then appear fighting, followed by Thersites, who calls them 'the cuckold and the cuckold-maker'. Left alone, Thersites is challenged by Margarelon, a bastard son of King Priam, but Thersites points out that he too is a bastard and bastards should not fight each other.

Scene eight Hector has captured the 'sumptuous armour' and killed its wearer. He disarms and sits down to rest. Achilles and his myrmidons discover him and at a word from Achilles, Hector, after objecting that he is unarmed, is slain. Trumpets sound from both armies to cease the action as night is falling and Achilles bids his men tie Hector's body to his horse's tail.

Scene nine The news that Achilles has slain Hector reaches the Greek commanders. Agamemnon suggests that this means that the Greeks have won and 'Great Troy' is theirs.

Scene ten The Trojans are rejoicing that they are 'masters of the field' (as the Greeks had rejoiced in the previous scene) when Troilus enters with the news that Hector is dead. He implies that this means the end of Troy but finishes his speech with the words: 'Hope of revenge shall hide our inward woe.' Pandarus enters, obviously hoping for a word with Troilus, but the latter spurns him contemptuously and departs. Pandarus is left to end the play with a pointless and not very elevating epilogue – as though Shakespeare himself was by now bored and disgusted with the whole thing.

VII Shakespeare's workmanship

The development of the story of Troilus and Cressida

Most of Shakespeare's plays show us the smooth, almost inevitable, development of the plot. The first act sets the scene, so to speak, introduces us to the principal characters and initiates the story. In act two the tension mounts and the story is taken a stage further. Act three brings a secondary climax, although sometimes (as in *Julius Caesar*) it seems to be a major crisis and the play threatens to fall away. Interest is skilfully kept alive in act four, which may also be a kind of calm before the storm. In act five the excitement mounts to the great scene where all problems are resolved, either happily or tragically.

Troilus and Cressida does not conform very closely to this pattern although it retains some of its elements, as the following analysis shows.

Act One *Scenes one and two: The love story*. We meet the lovers and are given a hint of Troilus's serious nature and Cressida's lightness.

The Trojan War. The Greek leaders are seen in conference. We gain some idea of the various characters but no very strong impression is left and nobody stands out as the probable 'hero' of the play. At the end of the act Hector's challenge to a single combat is received.

Act Two *The Trojan War*. In *scene one* we first learn of Achilles' pride and aloofness and in *scene two* there is a conference of the Trojan leaders. Hector emerges as at least a thoughtful character; even his apparent inconsistency is well reasoned – but so far there is little about him which is heroic. *Scene three* is taken up mostly by unimportant dissensions and schemes within the Greek headquarters.

Act Three *The love story*. We are reminded of Cressida's existence in *scene one*, and *scene two* shows us the lovers together. *Scene three* introduces the factor which is to shatter the idyll – the transfer of Cressida to the Greek camp. The last part of this scene, however, returns us to the Trojan War, or rather to the behaviour of the Greek leaders, especially in connection with the promised single combat.

Act Four *The love story. Scenes one and two* do little more than advance the matters of Cressida's return to her father and *scene three* is negligible, but there is an echo of *the Trojan War* in the talk about Helen in *scene one. Scene four* is all love story – the parting of Troilus and Cressida.

The Trojan War. Scene five begins with the love-story element in the arrival of Cressida in the Greek camp but passes to the War story with the promised Greek v. Trojan combat. This, however, itself comes to nothing.

Act Five *The Trojan War. Scene one* returns to the matter of the single combat.

The love story; Scene two: The end of the love story, when Troilus watches while Cressida betrays her vows to him.

The Trojan War. The rest of the play is about the war although nothing is settled. Hector emerges as the nearest to a hero the play has produced but the single combat never takes place; at one point both sides think they have won the war; and Troilus never wins back his Cressida or gets his revenge on the man who stole her.

It will be obvious from this skeleton outline that *Troilus and Cressida* is not a typical Shakespeare play. The love element comes to the surface every now and then but is hardly interlocked with the Trojan War element. Act five *appears* to run true to form in bringing things to a conclusion but close examination reveals that nothing is satisfactorily cleared up.

There may be several explanations of this comparative failure. For one thing Shakespeare derived his material from various different sources, each of which carried variations of both the love story and the political situation. If he failed to amalgamate his 'sources' as effectively as usual this is something we must accept; even Shakespeare could not always be at the top of his form. Another theory is that this play was written in two stages. We have seen (Section three) that there were two separate attributions of plays with this title by Shakespeare, with six years between them. It may well be that, in producing a play hurriedly for a special occasion in 1609, the author took the earlier play and added scenes or incidents to it without his usual care or skill. (In 1679 Dryden wrote an adaptation of the play which was very popular. His version re-arranges the incidents and makes various judicious 'cuts' but omits some of the finest poetry. Cressida, in Dryden's version, is faithful to Troilus but when he disbelieves her explanations she kills herself.)

Shakespeare's language

But after all, Shakespeare was Shakespeare. However feeble his plots – and there are one or two of his plays which are no more convincing in this respect than *Troilus and Cressida* – his language remains on the whole superb. Any playwright worth his salt can produce fine language to cope with an inspiring story or an exciting incident; it takes a genius to maintain a high level of expression when the inspiration and the excitement are lacking. It has been suggested – and some critics are more convinced about this than others – that not all of this play is the work of Shakespeare; if this is so it might explain some of the passages which fall below the general level; but on the whole the language is surely Shakespearean.

There are two great peaks, of course, and both are speeches by Ulysses. The first is spoken during the Greek conference in act one, scene three, where Ulysses pin-points the reasons, in his opinion, for the Greeks' failure to win this long drawn-out war. It is a plea for discipline, for the observance of 'degree' – the right relationship between the various ranks and 'classes'. The other is in act three, scene three, where Ulysses is giving sound but stern advice to Achilles, warning him not to trade on previous achievements but to keep his reputation steady and bright by constant endeavour.

Now *Troilus and Cressida* is not so conspicuous as the major comedies and tragedies for *imagery*, for the art of making an idea stand out almost startlingly by a sudden, unexpected comparison; yet these two speeches are full of it. In the earlier speech Ulysses says:

When that the general is not like the hive
To whom the foragers shall all repair,
What honey is expected?

The parallel with the world of bees was a popular gambit with all Elizabethan writers. Later he compares the position and influence of the general in an army with that of the sun, keeping in their positions all the 'planets' just as the good commander keeps his subordinates. 'Take but degree away', he says later, and then – another 'instant' metaphor – 'untune that string'; and this last metaphor leads to its extension – 'and hark what discord follows'. The second major speech is even more full of imagery; in fact it is almost one long extended metaphor. Achilles, snubbed by his fellow commanders in a previous scene, asks, 'What, are my deeds forgot? ' and Ulysses answers:

Time hath, my lord, a wallet at his back
Wherein he puts alms for oblivion

This means that Time is like a beggar who accepts alms but puts them in his wallet merely to be forgotten ('for oblivion'). 'Good deeds past' are 'forgotten soon as done'. In the rest of the speech, image follows image – a rusty nail in some travesty of a memorial; honour travelling in a path so narrow that only one (honour) can pass at a time; emulation (jealous rivalry) has a thousand sons who will overrun you and leave you behind; or leave you trodden underfoot like a horse that has fallen in the front rank . . . and so on. Perhaps the most arresting image is of the host, welcoming the incoming guest with open arms while looking over the departed guest's shoulder and offering him the most formal handshake.

But it is not only in the great set pieces that Shakespeare's genius shines. The love-crazed Troilus, in act three, scene two, says he is 'giddy' – 'expectation whirls me round'; Achilles (Act three, scene three) says:

My mind is troubled like a fountain stirred,
And I myself see not the bottom of it.

Troilus reproaches his brother Hector (Act five, scene three) for being too merciful with:

Let's leave the hermit pity with our mother;
And when we have our armours buckled on
The venomed vengeance ride upon our swords

Three images in three lines: pity as a hermit; vengeance as something poisoned; 'riding' on the sword.

At the other end of the scale we have the less attractive imagery of Thersites. He seldom speaks without using some surprising figure, usually something disgusting – at any rate to modern ears.

The greatness lies, partly at times, at times wholly, in the fact that we accept these images and comparisons almost without noticing them. Until we examined those three lines of Troilus's quoted above, we were probably not aware that there were three separate images; we recognized the idea of Pity as a hermit, but the other figures passed unnoticed. This again is a tribute to the poet's genius. He has lifted us to a plane on which imagery is accepted. People do not normally converse in blank verse; still less in rhymed couplets. When we hear or read dialogue in blank verse or rhyme written by an inferior poet or playwright we are aware of the anomaly; we complain to ourselves that this is not the way people talk. But with Shakespeare most of the time, and a few other playwrights occasionally, we make no such complaint; the poet has taken us along with him, especially when he varies the blank verse (and the words used) to suit the character who is speaking. It is because we have been transported in this way that we become accustomed to the use of imagery which would, indeed, strike us as excessive and unnatural in ordinary prose.

But imagery is not the whole picture; when we are considering Shakespeare's language we must also take into account his enormous vocabulary (which he is prepared to augment at any moment by the invention of a new word!); his vowel-play, which automatically and instinctively adds a so-called 'music' to his most poetic writing; his mastery of 'tone', which allows him to fit the speech to the speaker (e.g., Troilus nearly always *speaks* like a young man, Nestor like an old man); his ability to range at will from the pithy, almost over-compressed, to the long-winded. To isolate examples of all these (and other) skills would be too much like pulling a flower to pieces petal by petal to find where the scent comes from; moreover it would be doing too much for the student. This is pre-eminently the field in which the student must find his or her own treasures.

VIII Characterization

The *Dramatis Personae* of *Troilus and Cressida* usually divides the characters into Trojans and Greeks, with unattached or minor characters printed after the Greeks and the female characters last of all. In modern cast-lists for a stage performance the characters are more often printed 'in the order of their appearance' but this gives no indication of the characters' relative importance or even of the 'side' they are on. As the older practice places the Trojans first it will be convenient to adhere to that order.

Priam, king of Troy

As the Trojan War is little more than a background to the love-story and the personal dissensions and adventures of individual Trojan and Greek heroes, it is not surprising that we see little of King Priam. In act two, scene two, he presides over the 'conference' of his sons and asks their advice about returning Helen and so ending the war; but he makes no contribution of any importance to the debate. In act five, scene three, he is summoned by his daughter-in-law to support her and Cassandra in their efforts to persuade Hector not to fight on the day that was to prove fatal for him. Priam makes more or less formal protests but Hector is adamant and Priam bids him farewell, with a prayer for the gods' protection about him. In the last scene of the play Troilus asks who will break the news of Hector's death to Priam; it will turn the old man to stone, says Troilus.

Hector

One gets the feeling that Shakespeare would have liked to make Troilus the hero of this play but he was young and inexperienced – and too love-sick? – and the next best 'hero' was Troilus's older brother, Hector. He is brave and warlike and in both Classical and Elizabethan times was certainly regarded as an illustrious warrior and knight. We first meet him at the family conference in act two, scene two, where his attitude seems puzzling. He argues convincingly for the return of Helen to Menelaus, not so much to end the war but because it is right that a man should have his wife returned to him. (With Paris present it would have been tactless to insist that Helen should never have been 'stolen' in the first place.) Then, at the last moment, Hector changes sides. The chivalrous philosopher suddenly becomes the political opportunist. 'You're all wrong, theoretically,' he seems to say, 'but we can't let Helen go now without some loss of face, both individually and as a nation':

For 'tis a cause that hath no mean dependence
Upon our joint and several dignities.

No such indecision appears in the other actions and speeches of Hector. In act four he fights Ajax in single combat but his heart is obviously not in it. His excuse for withdrawing from the fight is that he cannot oppose his own nephew but it is more than likely that he suspected that Ajax had been 'chosen' to represent the Greeks partly as a snub to Achilles. We see his true valour in the last act, where he resists the appeals of his wife and his sister not to go to battle, spares Thersites as unworthy of his sword, kills Patroclus (off-stage) and is reported by Nestor as fighting everywhere ('There is a thousand Hectors in the field'). His killing of Patroclus arouses Achilles' wrath and ironically is the cause of his own death. After praising Troilus's efforts he encounters Achilles and they start to fight but he is disappointed to find that the Greek hero is less redoubtable than he expected. He offers to give the Greek 'a breather' and, after Achilles has ungraciously accepted his offer and left, Hector encounters another Greek, 'sumptuously armed'. He follows his victim and kills him for the sake of the armour – surely an uncharacteristic action. It is while he is resting, having taken off his armour, that Achilles finds him and treacherously has him killed. Achilles exacts the most humiliating revenge, according to Greek (and Elizabethan) ideas; he has Hector's body tied to his horse's tail and drags him away. In the last scene Troilus tells how the whole Trojan force will be dismayed by the news of Hector's death.

Shakespeare seems not to have completely made up his mind about Hector. If he needed a hero, here was the obvious choice for the part; but he is by no means perfect. In the very first act (scene two) we learn that, although with him patience was a 'fixed' virtue, he was so furious at being bettered by Ajax in a fight that he 'chid' his wife and even struck his armourer. His argument in the family conference is logical, well-balanced and persuasive yet at the end of it he changes his stand – as though, when it came to the pinch, chivalry and logic had to give way to expediency. But in the final count Shakespeare acknowledges him as his hero and gives him some of the finest verse to speak.

Troilus, Priam's youngest son

Troilus's love for Cressida provides more than half the plot, such as it is, of the play. His is a straightforward, almost a transparent, character. In the love scenes, especially in acts one and three, he speaks and feels like any young lover and his language is suitably poetic, even flowery. At the beginning he appears to be worshipping Cressida from afar, as unattainable, which is always the cue for extravagant and romantic talk. In act three, scene two, when he is apparently on the point of meeting Cressida for the first time, he can compare himself to a soul on the banks of Styx waiting to be ferried across ('staying for waftage'). When Pandarus goes to fetch her he tries to analyse his feelings and hopes he will not lose control of himself when he actually meets the girl. (Most young men, in such a position, would surely be inarticulate; they might whistle a tune or even, in a play, sing a song – anything but utter polished blank verse!) But when Cressida comes to him he speaks more sense, and he speaks in prose. When we next see Troilus, after his night with Cressida, he is speaking gently (and naturally) to her, but the news that she is to leave him for the Greek camp brings back his weakness for high-flown poetry, although as the parting draws near he returns to his more direct speech and even has an angry word for Diomedes. The scene (act five, scene two) where Troilus watches Cressida's flirtation with and surrender to Diomedes, again emphasizes Troilus's youthful immaturity. He keeps promising Ulysses that he will restrain himself – and keeps breaking his promise. A more mature, a more self-confident lover, one feels, would, at whatever risk, have dashed out and confronted the faithless Cressida and the seducer; but Troilus can only show a boyish lack of self-control and, after Cressida has gone, a futile but eloquent despair. We are never told how old Troilus was, but he must surely have been very young.

The loss of Cressida does not change Troilus; it merely brings out other aspects of his youthfulness. Rejected lovers have often threatened to commit suicide – although they seldom do so – and have thought they meant what they were saying. Troilus's way of seeking death is by feckless bravery on the battle-field. He rejects his brother Hector's advice to disarm and even rebukes him for his strain of mercifulness. He dashes into battle with a war-cry – 'I come to lose my arm, or win my sleeve', he utterly rejects Cressida's letter, whatever was in it; and although he fights Diomedes whenever he sees him he neither kills him nor is killed himself. In the end, in fact, he was as unsuccessful in war as he was in love; but his youth excuses him and we do not despise him. On the other hand, we cannot sympathize very deeply with him either. He impresses us as being in love with love more than with Cressida; he should have seen through her, or at least realized that the love-affair, such as it was, was the work of Pandarus rather than a spontaneous passion; and he seems to have accepted the loss of his beloved a little too easily, in a situation where words were not enough but deeds would have at any rate *looked* more earnest.

Paris

The second son of Priam was the legendary cause of the Trojan War since it was he who abducted Helen, the wife of Menelaus, king of Sparta; but his part in *Troilus and Cressida* is not important. He twice fights Menelaus; once in the first scene of the play, where we hear that he has been hurt; and again in act five, although we do not hear how this second encounter finishes. He takes part in the family discussion in act two, scene two and is not unexpectedly against returning Helen to her husband, but his argument is not very powerful. In act three, scene one, he appears with Helen. Pandarus has a message for him from Troilus but first Paris's servant and then Paris himself and Helen prevent him from delivering it and eventually force him to sing a love song. He flatters Helen and appears still to be in love with her ('Sweet, above thought I love thee.'). At the beginning of act four he challenges Diomedes to say who deserves Helen the more, he or Menelaus. Diomedes, a loyal Greek, has little good to say for Helen, to which Paris can only reply that Diomedes is like a merchant who denigrates something he wishes to buy (in the hope of getting the price reduced). He makes no further appearance of importance.

Deiphobus and **Helenus**

These two sons of Priam make more or less routine appearances whenever the Trojans are acting as a family or as a council of war. Deiphobus scarcely opens his mouth but Helenus, who is a priest, makes one speech during the debate on Helen, in favour of returning Helen to her husband. Troilus, with the impatience of youth, snubs him – 'You are for dreams and slumbers, brother priest.'

Margarelon

This son of Priam was a bastard. He appears only in the heat of battle in act five when he challenges Thersites, who avoids fighting by pointing out that he too is a bastard: 'One bear will not bite another, and wherefore should one bastard? '

Aeneas

This Trojan commander seems to be constantly appearing on the scene and yet somehow amounts to very little. In act one we learn that he has accompanied Troilus to the war and in scene three he brings Hector's challenge to single combat with the Greek's chosen champion. He is extremely polite and the perfect ambassador but the effect of his diplomacy is rather spoilt by the fact that he fails to recognize Agamemnon. In act four we meet him again, as suave and diplomatic as ever (although he warns Diomedes that he is a very different man when he is actually fighting!). It is he who has come to tell Troilus that Cressida is to be given back to her father in the Greek camp. He is present at the futile single combat and says all the right things when it is broken off. Finally he acts as a messenger and is present when Troilus announces the death of Hector.

Antenor

It is one of the ironies (unintentional?) of the play that this man never utters a word in it, because he is actually a very important Trojan commander. He had been captured by the Greeks, and the Trojans value him so highly that, to get him back, they are willing to exchange Cressida for him. Pandarus describes him, in act one, scene two, as 'one o'th' soundest judgements in Troy, and a proper man of person.' In fact he is never mentioned but in glowing terms although he never speaks.

Calchas

Calchas was a Trojan priest who, for reasons not disclosed, had gone over to the Greeks, leaving his daughter behind. He appears at the beginning of act three, when he asks the Greek commanders that, in return for services he has rendered them (not specified), he may have his daughter returned to him. He suggests that they exchange for her Antenor, captured only the day before, a commander whom the Trojans greatly prize. Agamemnon agrees. He is not present to greet her when she arrives and, as far as we know, makes no protest when she is apparently about to be seduced by Diomedes.

Pandarus

This comic figure was familiar to English people long before Shakespeare's day because of the word 'pander', derived from the same character in

Boccaccio and Chaucer. He is Cressida's uncle – but surely her mother's brother rather than her father's. We are not told what moved him to bring Cressida and Troilus together but in the earliest scenes of the play, and again in act three, scene two, this is his main preoccupation. In act two he points out to Cressida the Trojan heroes as they pass on their return from the battle and takes every opportunity to sing Troilus's praises. In act three, scene one he has an amusing encounter with Paris and Helen and in the next scene brings his self-imposed task with Cressida and Troilus to a successful conclusion. In act four he has the unpleasant job of learning from Aeneas that Cressida is to be returned to her father and of breaking the news to Cressida herself. Later he tries to console his niece. He makes no further contribution until the very end when he makes an ill-timed plea for Troilus's attention just after the latter has announced the death of Hector. Troilus spurns Pandarus with contempt and leaves him alone on the stage to speak the Epilogue (although it is not so named).

This 'epilogue' is something of a mystery; it is spoken by one of the less important characters; it makes no attempt to point a moral, to summarize or even to comment on what has happened in the play; and it is in a manner and tone which is not even typical of the speaker. It harps unpleasantly on venereal disease and implies that Pandarus himself is a victim; yet nowhere else in the play is this suggested. He is obviously an immoral – or at least amoral – manipulator, especially of Troilus but one feels he is more interested in bringing his scheme to a successful conclusion than in the physical sexual implications. He may carry about with him the atmosphere of the brothel but as a manager rather than an habitué. In Chaucer he was a kindly uncle-figure, anxious to do his niece and her lover a favour, and it is possible to see him still in this light in this play. But for Elizabethans he had become the lecherous go-between and his closing speech lives up – or down – to this image. It has been suggested with much plausibility, that the speech was added, by Shakespeare or another, when the play was to be performed more or less in private, since the tone would have been unacceptable to the general public, although the Elizabethan audiences had strong stomachs and would have been more likely to object to its irrelevance and its inaptness than to its immorality.

Agamemnon

When we pass to the Greeks we find some of the same enigmatic portraits as we found with the Trojans. Few characters are consistently straightforward, either one thing or the other. Dover Wilson maintains that the dominant note of *Troilus and Cressida* is satire and this would explain the tendency to denigrate the established figures and 'blow up' some of the less important, to find something faintly ridiculous where we were expecting to be impressed.

Agamemnon is not exactly a figure of fun, but neither is he the imposing figure the great Greek leader should surely have been. His first speech (act one, scene three), at the meeting of the Greek commanders, remains his best, but close examination shows that it contains little strong sense of leadership in a deal of high-flown language. Thereafter he appears in another four or five scenes but is ineffective. He fails in his attempt to 'discipline' Achilles and, most humiliating (and satirical?) blow of all, he is not recognized as the obvious commander-in-chief by the envoy, Aeneas (act one, scene three).

Menelaus

Menelaus was king of Sparta and presumably, as a king and the brother of Agamemnon, second-in-command of the Greeks. Helen, whose abduction by Paris started the war, was his wife and we twice see him fighting Paris personally. In the very first scene we learn from Aeneas that Paris has been wounded by Menelaus and in the last act the two of them are at it again. We are not told the outcome of this fight but as Menelaus appears two scenes later to hear of Hector's death, at least he was not killed. According to legend he was about to be slain when Venus intervened to save him; after all, it was he who chose her as the 'fairest' in the contest on Mount Ida.

Menelaus appears on stage frequently but seldom speaks.

Achilles

One of the most important characters of the play and one of the most baffling is Achilles. It is no exaggeration to say that it was his refusal to come out of his tent to join the fight which held up the Trojan War and robbed the Greeks of immediate victory. (We are not told *why* he sulked in his tent but the legend was that he had been deprived by Agamemnon of Briseis – later called Cressida – who had been his share of booty after a certain skirmish.) Ulysses speaks of him lying on his bed laughing at the 'scurrilous jests' and comic imitations of Greek generals offered by his friend Patroclus. When Hector's challenge to single combat with any representative the Greeks might choose is first brought, it is assumed that Achilles will be the man. But Ulysses has a plan to put Ajax in Achilles' place as a snub (see Ajax, below) and the other leaders fall in with his plan (act one, scene three, last eighty lines). In act three, scene three, the Greek leaders continue their plan to humiliate Achilles by walking past him and more or less ignoring him, but Ulysses stays behind and lectures Achilles in a firm but friendly way. Achilles is not disposed to alter his ways but he is anxious to meet Hector, unarmed, after the single combat. He is in the gathering which welcomes Cressida in act four, scene five, and greets her with a kiss. He watches the futile combat and, after it, meets Hector and arranges for them to duel the next day. But almost immediately (act five, scene one) he receives a letter from Queen Hecuba, Hector's mother, reminding him of his vows to Polyxena, Hector's sister; honour binds him to keep his vow, which means that he cannot fight Hector – surely another satirical touch: that the great Achilles could be deflected from an undertaking to fight – and presumably to kill – a deadly rival by a vow made to an absent mistress whom we have not heard of before in the play.

But the reluctant Achilles is at last moved to violent action by the news that his friend Patroclus has been killed – and by Hector himself. He angrily arms himself and dashes into the battle. But the long spell of inaction has told on him and he is unable to maintain the fight when he at last meets Hector. The Trojan allows him to escape but Achilles comes upon him when he is resting and unarmed. His myrmidons – wild Greek mercenaries whom Achilles had brought to Troy – kill Hector and Achilles inflicts the final degradation on the corpse.

It is difficult to 'fix' the image of Achilles in this play. In act one, scene two, Pandarus calls him 'a drayman, a porter, a very camel'; but Pandarus is prepared to run down Achilles in order to raise Troilus in Cressida's eyes. In the next scene Ulysses, before he complains of Achilles' inactivity refers to him as 'The great Achilles, whom opinion crowns / the sinew and the forehand of our host' – but he again may be praising Achilles in order to increase the force of the attack on him which he is planning. His behaviour throughout the play is certainly not that of a great national hero; his sulky inactivity and foolish trifling with Patroclus strike us as childish; his furious activity after the death of Patroclus was, to say the least, intemperate. As for the treacherous murder of Hector, this seems the most unworthy action of all. If Shakespeare was intending to satirize the Greeks he could not have done a better job with Achilles.

Ajax

Ajax was another victim of Shakespeare's irony. In act one, scene two Alexander, Cressida's servant, gives a clever description of Ajax as a mixture of opposites, ending: 'everything so out of joint that he is a gouty Briareus, many hands and no use, or a purblind Argus, all eyes and no sight'. To some extent Shakespeare was helped by an Elizabethan pun, 'a jakes' being the popular term for a privy. He certainly made the most of it. In act two, scene three Ulysses plays him like an angler with an unusually stupid fish. The other Greeks support Ulysses, either in the presence of Ajax himself or in his absence. Ajax, in fact, is led to think he is the obvious opponent for Hector in the approaching single combat but in act four, scene five, when the combat at last takes place, he meekly accepts Hector's suggestion to stop the fight since he and Ajax are related. In the general battle in act five both he and Diomedes are taken on by Troilus and although we never learn how that fight ends we are told later that 'Ajax hath ta'en Aeneas'.

Shakespeare's Ajax is a sort of combination of Homer's and Ovid's. He was said to be physically heavy and mentally slow-witted but he was never quite the vain, blustering fool of *Troilus and Cressida.*

Ulysses

At first Ulysses seems to be the one character who is consistent. His speech on 'degree' to the Greek council is wise and well argued. His plan to trick Achilles into action by making him jealous of Ajax (act one, scene three) is clever and skilfully carried out (it was not Ulysses' fault that it was not successful). His long speech of advice to Achilles (act three, scene three), with its sting in the tail about Polyxena, is one of the high-lights of the play. So far, at least, Shakespeare seems to approve of Ulysses since he has given him the best speeches in the play. But as the play goes on we begin to wonder. In act four, scene five he is among the Greeks who welcome Cressida back and begs a kiss, like the rest (it is not clear whether he gets it!) but the moment she has gone he tears her character to pieces. He had not much evidence but his attack would be popular with the Elizabethan audience who thought of Cressida as a harlot. In act five, scene two, he takes Troilus to a spot where they can witness the rejection of Troilus by Cressida in favour of Diomedes. Why should he do this? Although he tries to restrain Troilus it seems that this is not out of any sympathy but rather that he fears they will be discovered. He seems almost unable to understand what Troilus is upset about and his attempt to console Troilus after Cressida has gone seems strangely formal. We meet him briefly again in act five when he comes to announce that Achilles is at last arming himself for battle.

It has been said that Ulysses is cold and calculating but trivial-minded; his grandiloquent theories are not supported by his actions. This is surely too strong a judgement. The fact remains that Ulysses proves a disappointment. He was clearly not a fighting man but if his counsels had been consistently as high-minded as were the finest of his speeches he might have been of inestimable value to the Greeks.

Nestor

Nestor is the oldest of the Greek leaders. The others usually treat him with respect – apart from Thersites who calls him (act five, scene four) 'that stale old mouse-eaten dry cheese'. He himself regrets his age when he meets Hector (act four, scene five) ('By this white beard, I'ld fight with thee tomorrow' adding, with a sigh, 'I have seen the time.') He enters into Ulysses' plan to arouse Achilles; he is among the first to welcome Cressida with a kiss, in fact, for an old man, he is constantly active. But he has little if anything to do or say which affects the play to any serious extent.

Diomedes

In Homer, Diomedes was a very important warrior, second only to Achilles; Shakespeare gives him a comparatively small part, but it is an extremely important one. Agamemnon sends him to bring back Cressida and when they arrive in the Greek camp she is given into his care, although she was supposed to have been sent to her father, who had pleaded to have her back. He soon discovers that Cressida is 'easy game' and wins her over with indecent speed. His cynical – or clear-sighted – assessment of Cressida is matched by his view of Helen (act four, scene one), expressed with utter frankness – and to Paris of all people.

He apparently takes little part in the war until act five, where he has two fights with Troilus in the first of which he captures Troilus's horse, which he sends as a gift to Cressida.

As we watch Diomedes' all-too-easy conquest of Cressida we are reminded of Troilus's pregnant question in the early debate on Helen: 'What's aught but as 'tis valued? ' Diomedes' success supplies a far clearer answer than that which Ulysses, with his touch of philosophy, had given at the time.

Patroclus

Until the last Act, Patroclus never appears without Achilles or Thersites; often he appears with both. As one of the Greek commanders he was of equal rank with Achilles and they were obviously great friends, but one gets the impression that Achilles was the leading spirit. We first hear of him in Ulysses' account of Achilles lying in his tent (act one, scene three) being entertained by Patroclus; Ulysses seems to admit, however grudgingly, that he is a good mimic. From time to time, it appears, Patroclus has tried to persuade Achilles to take up arms again, but without success. It is not until he is killed, by Hector, that Achilles is at last stung into action. His part in *Troilus and Cressida* is not in itself of great importance but he throws some light on the charachter of Achilles.

Thersites

If Achilles' frivolous time-wasting with Patroclus can be excused, or at least explained, by the fact that they were fellow commanders, no such excuse can be put forward for Achilles' toleration of Thersites. He is deformed in body and in mind, foul in his language, obsessed with loathsomeness in the spirit and the flesh, concerned only to reduce humanity to the level of the beasts. We meet him first in act two, scene one, where he vents his spleen on Ajax – Achilles is said to have 'stolen' Thersites from Ajax, who is certainly more free with his sword or his fists than Achilles – and refuses to be tamed. In act two, scene three he rails first at Ajax and Achilles then at Agamemnon and when Patroclus intervenes Achilles says: 'He is a privileged man. Proceed, Thersites.' In the next scene but one, when Achilles wants a letter taken to Ajax and Patroclus more or less refuses to take it, Thersites gets the job but in a short speech before he leaves shows that he has no illusions about Achilles. In act five, scene one, it is he who brings Achilles the letter from Hecuba which makes him change his mind about fighting Hector after which he renews his attack on Agamemnon and later on Menelaus and then Diomedes. (In this and other scenes he reveals his other obsession, animals. His most frequent allusions are to dogs, horses, toads, lizards – usually in their least pleasant aspects – and even lice!) He accompanies Ulysses and Troilus when they spy on Cressida and Diomedes and his asides are sharp, scurrilous and sometimes obscene. At the end of the scene he returns to his other obsession: 'Lechery, lechery! Still wars and lechery! Nothing else holds fashion.' He is frightened to death when he meets Hector on the war-path but again drags lechery into his outburst.

There is nothing likeable about Thersites but he is not without shrewdness. He is not far wrong, for example, when he blames the whole Trojan War on lechery, even if he carried this conviction too far and let it colour his whole view of life; and there is some truth in many of the slanderous things he has to say about some of the leaders on both sides. Perhaps his greatest significance is that he is a glaring illustration of that absence of discipline and 'degree' in the Greek camp to which Ulysses attributed, early in the play, the lack of success of the Greek army. If such a disreputable and scurrilous hanger-on can be tolerated, even encouraged, by leaders like Achilles and Patroclus there must be something wrong with the 'tone' of the Greek army.

Alexander

Alexander is Cressida's servant and makes only one appearance when, in act one, he gives her a remarkable summary of the character of Ajax and tells of Hector's uncharacteristic anger at being worsted by Ajax in battle. Shakespeare seems occasionally to 'forget' a character after a single early appearance. The interesting thing is that he sometimes gives this 'one-appearance' character some extremely well-written lines to speak.

Troilus and Cressida must be discouraging for a girls' school or a women's college looking for a play to perform in public. There are only four female characters, of whom one, Helen, must be outstandingly beautiful. She, and two of the other three, make only a few brief appearances and are of minor significance in the play. The fourth, however, is what actors call a 'fat' part.

Cressida

It is necessary to bear in mind the popular image of Cressida in Shakespeare's time. Chaucer's Cryseyde was a gentle, kind and serious girl; Henryson's Cresseid was a wanton, rejected by Diomedes when he discovered her real character, and abandoned, to become a leper and a beggar. Henryson's version was the more recent and the word 'cressida' almost became a synonym for 'strumpet', just as the word 'greek' came to mean 'cunning' or 'cheating'. Shakespeare spared his audience the last stages of Cressida's disintegration but he left them in no doubt that she was, at the best, faithless.

When we first meet her, with her servant Alexander, she seems a normal, not unintelligent young woman who hardly seems to realize that Pandarus, when he comes on the scene, is 'pushing' Troilus for all he's worth. But after Pandarus has gone she admits that she has seen what he was driving at and already admires Troilus. But she resolves not to give herself away – yet – and rather glibly concludes that 'Men prize the thing ungained more than it is.' In what might well be her first encounter with Troilus (act three, scene two) she begins almost modestly but soon agrees to fall in with Pandarus's plan for her seduction, although she pretends to blame Pandarus ('what folly I commit, I dedicate to you').

On the very next day she hears she is to be sent to her father and the Greeks and her distress seems quite genuine, as do her protestations of love and fidelity to Troilus (act four, scene four), but in the next scene, when she is introduced to the Greek commanders, she seems to have recovered her composure and holds her own in any contest of wit. (It is worth noting that the commanders – even old Nestor – have no hesitation in greeting her with a kiss. Whether this was a token of their belief that she was 'anybody's girl', or whether Shakespeare merely sought to create the impression of a wanton remains a moot point.) In the scene (act five, scene two) where she yields to Diomedes she really discloses her true nature. She has already promised Diomedes some favour – on the way from the Trojan camp, presumably – for he asks her to keep her promise and she pretends to be coy – 'I prithee, do not hold me to mine oath; / Bid me do anything but that, sweet Greek'. But she knows how to lead him on until the time is ripe and she fetches the sleeve that Troilus had given her. Still she appears to be holding back – or is it a twinge of conscience? – and says 'He loved me – O false wench! – Give't me again.' Her little soliloquy when Diomedes has gone, with her promise to come to him still in his ears, does nothing to redeem her; the best she can do is to blame her sex and the evil power of the eyes.

This is the last we see of Cressida but Shakespeare has done his work well. He has changed the charm of Chaucer's Cryseyde into the lust of Henryson's Cresseid but kept enough of her earlier appearance of ignorance to make us wonder, at first, whether she was, or wanted to be, a 'good girl' – enough at least to make us feel a little sympathy for her. We know, with hindsight, that she was playing on Troilus's inexperience and his infatuation but at the time she persuaded Troilus, herself and even us that she genuinely loved the handsome young Troilus – or did she?

IX Essay topics

The following are some typical questions which might be asked on *Troilus and Cressida* at Matriculation or School Certificate or O level standard. It must be stressed again, however, that a thorough knowledge of the text of the play itself is essential and that these questions are not to be considered as likely 'spots'.

1. Choose *eight* of the following extracts and for each extract state: (a) by whom, to whom, and under what circumstances each was spoken, and (b) the general meaning of the extract and its special significance in the development of the play:

(i) *I stalk about her door,*
Like a strange soul upon the Stygian banks
Staying for waftage. O, be thou my Charon,
And give me swift transportance to those fields
Where I may wallow in the lily beds
Proposed for the deserver!

(ii) *Ajax hath lost a friend,*
And foams at mouth, and he is armed and at it,
Roaring for Troilus; who hath done today
Mad and fantastic execution,
Engaging and redeeming of himself
With such a careless force and forceless care
As if that luck, in very spite of cunning,
Bade him win all.

(iii) *O, let not virtue seek*
Remuneration for the thing it was;
For beauty, wit,
High birth, vigour of bone, desert in service,
Love, friendship, charity, are subject all
To envious and calumniating Time.

(iv) *For every false drop in her bawdy veins*
A Grecian's life hath sunk; for every scruple
Of her contaminated carrion weight
A Trojan hath been slain; since she could speak,
She hath not given so many good words breath
As for her Greeks and Trojans suffered death.

(v) *Why, have you any discretion? have you any eyes? do you know what a man is? Is not birth, beauty, good shape, discourse, manhood, learning, gentleness, virtue, youth, liberality, and such like, the spice and salt that season a man?*

(vi) *If beauty have a soul, this is not she;*
If souls guide vows, if vows be sanctimonies,
If sanctimony be the gods' delight,
If there be rule in unity itself,
This is not she.

(vii) *'Tis like he'll question me*
Why such unplausive eyes are bent on him.
If so, I have derision medicinable
To use between your strangeness and his pride,
Which his own will shall have desire to drink.

(viii) A. *He that is proud eats up himself: pride is his own glass, his own trumpet, his own chronicle; and whatever praises itself but in the deed, devours the deed in the praise.*

B. *I do hate a proud man as I do hate the engendering of toads.*

C (aside) *And yet he loves himself: Is is not strange?*

(ix) *I must not believe you.*
There they stand yet; and modestly I think
The fall of every Phrygian stone will cost
A drop of Grecian blood. The end crowns all;
And that old common arbitrator, Time,
Will one day end it.

(x) *the bounded waters*
Should lift their bosoms higher than the shores,
And make a sop of all this solid globe;
Strength should be lord of imbecility,
And the rude son should strike his father dead.

(xi) *Hark! you are called. Some say the Genius so*
Cries 'Come! ' to him that instantly must die.

(xii) *The dragon wing of night o'erspreads the earth,*
And stickler-like the armies separates.
My half-supped sword that frankly would have fed,
Pleased with this dainty bait, thus goes to bed.

(xiii) *His stubborn buckles,*
With these your white enchanting fingers touched,
Shall more obey than to the edge of steel
Or force of Grecian sinews.

(xiv) *We turn not back the silks upon the merchant*
When we have soiled them; nor the remainder viands
We do not throw in unrespective sieve
Because we now are full.

(xv) *The elephant hath joints, but none for courtesy:*
his legs are legs for necessity, not for flexure.

(xvi) A. *Fly not; for shouldst thou take the river Styx,*
I would swim after.

B. *Thou dost miscall retire;*
I do not fly; but advantageous care
Withdrew me from the odds of multitude.

2. In the first Folio, *Troilus and Cressida* is placed between the Comedies and the Tragedies. To which category, in your opinion, does it more rightly belong?

3. Give in your own words as far as possible an account of the encounter in act three, scene one between Pandarus, Paris and Helen.

4. What evidence do you find in the play that Shakespeare had a satirical purpose in writing *Troilus and Cressida*?

5. How far do you agree with the suggestion that, in *Troilus and Cressida*, Shakespeare failed to link effectively the two threads of his story – the Trojan War and the love-story?

6. Compare and contrast the characters, language and actions of Pandarus and Thersites, with special reference to the importance of these characters in the working out of such plot as there is.

7. Comment on (i) the different styles and qualities of the blank verse in this play and (ii) Shakespeare's use of prose for some of the scenes.

8. On page 7 of this book (section two) it is suggested that we know some of the characters in a play by what other characters say about them, as well as by their own speeches and actions. *Troilus and Cressida* is more full than most plays of this kind of information and illumination by 'other characters'. Give some examples of this and say how far the information so conveyed is either reliable or helpful.

9. Compare Agamemnon and Priam as leaders of their respective forces.

10. Relate, in your own words as far as possible, the events strictly connected with the war as they are presented to us in act five.

11. How far, in your opinion, was Troilus responsible for his own troubles?

12. '*Troilus and Cressida* ends without a climax or a resolution.' Comment on this statement and suggest any reasons you can to account for this disappointing ending.

13. Discuss the importance in the play of (a) Menelaus and (b) Ajax. N.B. You are not asked to write a character-sketch of either.

14. *Troilus and Cressida* has been described as 'a history without dignity, a comedy without laughter and a tragedy without tears'. Comment on this description, showing how far you agree with it (or disagree with it), giving reasons for your decisions.

15. When we speak of the 'hero' of a play we mean either a central, commanding figure or a brave, heroic man. Which characters qualify for the role of 'hero' in this play, under either qualification?

16. What are the outstanding differences of character and temperament between the Greeks, taken as a whole, and the Trojans? How does Shakespeare bring out these differences?

17. Why do you think *Troilus and Cressida* is usually classed as one of Shakespeare's 'problem' plays?

18. Write an assessment of Ulysses and of his importance in the play.

(Wherever appropriate, your answers to these questions should be supported by quotation. In any case, *close reference* to the text is essential.)

Key to Question 1 (In some cases the *line* reference may be only approximate, particularly if the extract is in prose or from a scene partly written in prose.)

(i)	Act three,	scene 2;	lines 7– 12
(ii)	Act five,	scene 5;	lines 35– 42
(iii)	Act three,	scene 3;	lines 169–174
(iv)	Act four,	scene 1;	lines 71– 76

(v)	Act one,	scene 2;	lines 252–256
(vi)	Act five,	scene 2;	lines 138–142
(vii)	Act three,	scene 3;	lines 42– 46
(viii)	Act two,	scene 3;	lines 153–159
(ix)	Act four,	scene 5;	lines 221–226
(x)	Act one,	scene 3;	lines 111–115
(xi)	Act four,	scene 4;	lines 50– 51
(xii)	Act five,	scene 8;	lines 17– 20
(xiii)	Act three,	scene 1;	lines 151–154
(xiv)	Act two,	scene 2;	lines 69– 72
(xv)	Act two,	scene 3;	lines 104–105
(xvi)	Act five,	scene 4;	lines 18– 21

X Reading list

Text

The *Arden* edition of Shakespeare's plays (Methuen) is scholarly and readable, if *Troilus and Cressida* is available in this edition. The *New Cambridge* edition, in hard cover or paper-back (Cambridge University Press) has valuable introductory essays, with good notes and glossary. The *Troilus and Cressida* in this edition is perhaps not so interesting as that of most of the plays but is vaulable for its account of the sources, background and historical information.

Between school and university editions the American *Signet* is illuminating and has the essential Notes (including vocabulary) at the foot of each page. There are many school editions of the plays but few of *Troilus and Cressida*. Handy 'pocket' editions, for reading rather than study, are the *Penguin* and Dent's *Temple* Shakespeare.

Shakespeare's life and times

Life in Shakespeare's England, edited by J. Dover Wilson (Penguin paper-back; Cambridge University Press hard cover). A fascinating anthology from many contemporary sources.
Shakespeare's England (Oxford University Press). A large two-volume collection of scholarly essays on every aspect of Elizabethan life and culture, with many illustrations.
Life in Tudor England by Penry Williams (Batsford). A well-illustrated description of the changes in English society during the sixteenth century.
Shakespeare and his Stage by Marchette Chute (University of London Press). A biography with descriptions of London and Stratford life.

General studies of Shakespeare's plays

Introducing Shakespeare by G.B. Harrison (Penguin)
Approach to Shakespeare by Derek Traversi (Sands)
Shakespeare's Bawdy by Eric Partridge (Routledge)
The Development of Shakespeare's Imagery by Wolfgang Clemen (Methuen: University Paperback 171)
The Language of Shakespeare's Plays by Ifor Evans (Methuen: University Paperback 113)

Criticism of 'Troilus and Cressida'

Shakespeare's Problem Plays by E.M.W. Tillyard (Chatto & Windus)
The Wheel of Fire by G. Wilson Knight (Oxford University Press)
The Frontiers of Drama by Una Ellis-Fermor (Methuen)